Growing up in
THE EIGHTEENTH
CENTURY

Nance Lui Fyson

B. T. Batsford Ltd *London*

© Nance Lui Fyson 1977

First published 1977
Second impression 1984

ISBN 0 7134 0481 7

Printed and bound in Great Britain
by Anchor Brendon Ltd, Tiptree, Essex
for the Publishers B T Batsford Limited
4 Fitzhardinge Street, London W1H 0AH

Frontispiece **'Marianne' by W Wynne Ryland, 1780**

Acknowledgment

The Author and Publishers thank the following for
their kind permission to reproduce copyright
illustrations: the Trustees of the British Museum for
fig 3; A F Kersting for figs 24 and 26; the Mansell
Collection for figs 1, 2, 4, 8, 11, 13, 15, 18, 21, 28,
31, 36, 43, 46-8 and 56; the National Museum of
Wales for fig 20; the Radio Times Hulton Picture
Library for the frontispiece and figs 5-7, 12, 14, 16,
17, 19, 22, 32, 35, 37-8, 40, 42, 49, 50, 52, 54-5,
and 57-8; the Science Museum for fig 45; and the
Victoria and Albert Museum for fig 51. The other
illustrations appearing in the book are the property
of the Publishers.

Contents

The Illustrations

1 The Georgian Age

The eighteenth century was a time of great changes in Britain. In the early 1700s most of the people lived in villages and quiet country towns. But by the 1760s the age of the Industrial Revolution had begun, and people began to move into the towns to work in the factories. New farming methods were discovered which made the old ways of farming (in small strips of land) seem inefficient. As men became rich from industry, they bought up land, and enclosed it in large fields. They even enclosed common land so that the poor could not use it, and had to turn to industry to earn a living.

Against this background of social change, the Georgian Age flourished as a time of cultural elegance and imperialist expansion. Queen Anne (reign: 1702-14) was the last of the House of Stuart. The Georgian Age spanned the reigns of George I (1714-27), George II (1727-60), George III (1760-1820) and George IV (1820-30) of the House of Hanover. During this time, Britain grew from being a small commercial and sea-faring state into a great and powerful empire, with colonies in America and Australia.

Children growing up in the early part of the century did not have much freedom, but later in the century a new attitude towards children began to grow. 'The earliest lives I have found of children who may not have been beaten at all date from 1690 to 1750' (Lloyd de Mause, *The History of Childhood*). Pictures painted after 1730 show more and more children playing or fishing or having a picnic with their parents.

1 & 2 The painting below, by William Hogarth, shows children as little adults — which is how they were dressed and regarded in 1730. Gradually over the century children were less restrained. The painting overleaf (by H. Robinson, 1782) shows a boy flying a kite. How much freer he seems.

By the 1740s (at least among the middle and upper classes) there was a somewhat freer and more gentle treatment of children.

However, the eighteenth century was a violent age, and children were often treated very badly. Very young children were expected to work long hours, and punishments for disobedience were harsh. Violence was commonplace in the towns. When a move was made to install better street lighting in Cambridge, people worried that men would fight each other instead of passing each other unrecognized!

3 This 1718 street scene by Hogarth shows typical aspects of town life. The sign above the barber's shop reads 'Shaving, Bleeding and Teeth Drawn at a Touch'. Children sleep in the street, a chamber pot is emptied on the heads of passers-by, while a coach is being overturned and robbed by thieves.

6

2 Children at Work

In the early eighteenth century 'work for children' meant mainly temporary and seasonal odd jobs in the fields, for example, stone picking, bird scaring, collecting mushrooms or blackberries. Industrialization in the second half of the century changed all this. Many children were forced to work in cotton mills and coal mines. Even children of four or five worked 12 or more hours a day. In 1810 the total labour force of 350,000 included 101,000 children.

The beginnings of the Industrial Revolution were earlier than 1750, but change was very fast from 1780 on. Machines for spinning and weaving were invented. The steam engine was developed. Factories grew, mainly in Lancashire and Yorkshire. The coal mining and iron industries also grew rapidly.

Textiles was the biggest industry, after agriculture. In the early part of the century textiles was a cottage industry. It was part of the 'domestic system'. Men and women spun and wove in their homes. Clothiers sold them raw materials, bought their finished goods, and rented them looms. (There were some other industries as well on the domestic system, such as nail-making, glove-making, stocking-making).

Lace-making, straw-plaiting, and button-making were some domestic industries using children. At four years old children sorted straws; they plaited at five, and earned a small wage at six. Three and four year old children were taught to use bobbins. One child was reported to have started work

4   Factory children going to work in Yorkshire in 1814.

5 Rope-making in 1754. Children are working with adults in the complex twisting of rope. Children helped with many industries of this kind.

One eighteenth century writer recalled helping as a child in the family cottage workshop:

drawing lace at age two. At the age of four the child worked 12 hours a day, with less than an hour for meals.

At one Northamptonshire lace school, the hours were from 6am to 6pm in the summer and from 8am to 8pm in the winter. The girls had to stick ten pins a minute. They worked only half a day on Saturdays. They could earn about 6d (2½p) a day. In the day-time as many as 30 girls, sometimes boys, would work in a room about 12 feet (4 metres) square with only two windows. In the winter they would have no fire for lack of room.

I recollect that soon after I was able to walk I was employed in the cotton manufacture. My mother used to bat the cotton wool on a wire riddle. It was then put into a deep brown mug with a strong ley of soap suds. My mother then tucked up my petticoats about my waist, and put me into the tub to tread upon the cotton at the bottom. When a second riddleful was batted I was lifted out, it was placed in the mug, and I again trod it down. This process was continued until the mug became so full that I could no longer safely stand in it, when a chair

was placed beside it and I held on by the back. When the mug was quite full, the soap suds were poured off, and each separate dollop of wool well squeezed to free it from moisture. They were then placed on the bread rack under the beams of the kitchen to dry. My mother and my grandmother carded the cotton wool by hand, taking one of the dollops at a time, on the single hand cards. When carded they were put aside in separate parcels ready for spinning. (French, *Life of Crompton*)

The new machinery and new factories gradually stopped this domestic system. It became cheaper to have the work done in the factories. Handloom weaving continued in homes at least until 1850 — but on a very small scale, and it no longer offered a living wage. The cotton industry adopted the new machines more easily than the woollen industry.

The cotton mills
The growth of cotton mills meant a big change in the working conditions of spinners

6 Children winding cotton. Textile mills made use of much child labour — often in hard and unsafe conditions.

and weavers. While they worked in their own cottages they could set conditions for themselves. The mill owners ran a harsh system of discipline. The hours were long and holidays were few. There were fines for lateness, talking at work, or opening a window. The machines were very noisy. The atmosphere was kept hot and moist to keep the cotton threads from snapping when they were stretched.

Large numbers of women and children worked at the mills. This was because they could be paid lower wages than men, and their nimble fingers were useful for delicate threading among the machinery. In 1816 the mills of Manchester employed twice as many women as men, and nearly as many children as adults. Earlier, the proportion of children was even higher. The first cotton mills made use of pauper apprentices. Thousands of pauper children were sent by waggon or barge from London and other large towns. They were fed, clothed, and lodged in houses by their employers. The children were worked very hard and beaten to keep them in line. They were locked up at night to keep them from running away. When the day was over, overseers made the rounds of the mills to collect those children that had fallen asleep in corners, exhausted.

Robert Blincoe, who was born about 1792, was put in St Pancras workhouse when he was a child. A cotton-factory owner near Nottingham asked for some new apprentices, and some of the children, including Robert, were sent from the workhouse. The children were deliberately misled. They were told they were going to a wonderful place, where they would be fed roast beef and plum-pudding. Their lives at the mill were in fact quite awful. They had watery porridge and doughy black bread

for supper. A large man with a horse-whip kept them in order.

Blincoe later reported that he was sent to a room where he was told to pick up the loose cotton. Not used to the stench and dust and terrified by the machinery, he soon felt very ill, and his back ached. About the second year Blincoe was at the mill a terrible accident happened. A girl, Mary Richards, about ten years old, had her apron caught in some machinery she was working. Blincoe heard her shrieks. He saw her whirled round with the shaft. The bones of her body were crushed as the machinery whirled her round. Her blood streamed upon the floor. When she was finally taken out, every bone in her body was broken and her head was crushed. But she was somehow saved, and sent back to work at the very same mill, a cripple for life.

Blincoe also reported on the living conditions. The apprentices slept about 50 in a room. On Sunday, bacon-broth and turnips were served out in dirty wooden bowls. There was usually some broth left over. In this hog-wash more water was poured and some meal stirred in. This mess was to be supper or the next day's breakfast. Blincoe said that the smell of the broth turned his stomach, and yet he was so starved that he ate it. When they had rice pudding the rice was bad and full of maggots. The work, filth, and hunger led to many fevers among the children.

The master of the factory knocked down children with clenched fists, beat them with sticks or whips. They were raised by the ears, lifted and forcibly dashed to the floor. They would be pinched until his nails met!

There were a few cases in which the mill children were treated better. A 1780 mill built by Samuel Oldknow at Mellor had a pleasant apprentice house where the children were well fed and educated.

A number of eighteenth-century writers mentioned childrens' work and wages. Arthur Young in *A Six Week's Tour*

Through the Counties of England and Wales wrote that at Rotherham:

Those boys of fourteen and over earned from 3s to 4s a week. Boys of nine and ten years old earned 2s and 2s 6d a week at the pottery. . . In the plated work some hundreds of hands are employed; girls earn 4s 6d and 5s a week; some even to 9s . . . Here is likewise a silk mill, which employs 152 hands, chiefly women and children; the women earn 5s or 6s a week by the pound; girls at first are paid but 1s or 1s 2d a week.

Arthur Young noted that the wages of 'a lad of 13 or 14 years old' working on a farm were 4d a day. Daniel Defoe in *A Tour thro the Island of Great Britain* wrote:

We came to Taunton. . . One of the chief Manufacturers here told us that they had eleven hundred Looms going for the weaving of Sagathies, Duroys, and Such Kind of Stuffs; He added, That there was not a Child in the Town or in the Villages round it, of above five Years old, but if it was not neglected by its Parents, and untaught, could earn its own Bread.

At the beginning of the nineteenth century there grew a concern for the very poor treatment of children in mills. The Health and Morals of Apprentices Act 1802 limited the working day of pauper apprentices in cotton mills to 12 hours. It forbade night work and required daily teaching. The Cotton Factory Act of 1819 applied to all children working in mills. It forbade their employment before the age of 9 and limited the working day of children aged 9 to 16 to 10½ hours. This was difficult to enforce and many factories did not follow it.

The Factory Act of 1833 limited the labour of children aged 9 to 13 in textile mills to 48 hours a week, and not more than 9 hours a day. Those under 18 were limited to 68 hours a week and not more than 12 hours a day. Factory inspectors were appointed to enforce this.

Mining

Children in mines also worked long hard days. Girls as well as boys were set to work at age five or six as 'trappers'. Fresh air was let into the mines by a series of doors which had to be opened and shut every time a load of coal was drawn along. For 12 hours a day, often in complete darkness, the trappers sat huddled against the doors ready to pull them open as the coal appeared. 'I'm a trapper in the Gauber Pit' said a little girl aged eight. 'I have to trap without a light, and I'm scared. I go at four, and sometimes half-past three in the morning, and come out five and half-past. . .'

Older children in the mines became 'fillers'. Their job was to fill the tubs or corves as the coal was cut from the seams. The loaded trucks were then pushed or pulled to the bottom of the pit shaft by other boys and girls called 'pushers' or 'hurriers'. They were harnessed to the trucks by means of a belt to which a chain from the carriage was hooked and passed between their legs. In some mines the height of the roof was only 60cm (24 inches), and in some cases 45cm (18 inches). Patience Kershaw's task was to push loaded tubs:

I hurry in the clothes I have now got on (trousers and ragged jacket). The bald

7 This old print of children working in a coal mine shows what it was like for the 'trappers' who opened doors and the 'hurriers' who pushed heavy loads in the grim, unhealthy pits.

place upon my head is made by thrusting the corves. I hurry the corves a mile or more underground and back; they weigh 3cwt. I hurry 11 hours a day. I wear a belt and chain at the workings to get the corves out. The getters that I work for sometimes beat me if I am not quick enough.

Chimney sweeps

There were other trades in which eighteenth-century children were employed. Chimney sweeps made use of small boys. They were likely to be burned, stifled, or stuck half-way up the chimney if care was not taken. These boys were kept half-starved so they would be thin enough to do their work, and many contracted cancer as a result of their working conditions.

The chimney sweep boys were usually supplied by the parish authorities. In 1767 and 1778 laws were passed laying down that premiums paid for the boys must be in two instalments. Thus sweeps needed to keep the boys alive for at least several years. Children were sometimes stolen from parents to sell as chimney sweeps.

Thick layers of soot encrusted the faces and bodies of these children. They were rarely washed. The small boys (sometimes girls) slept in cellars on sacks of soot. Sometimes they were forced to climb not only to sweep the chimney, but to put out a fire. They might have to climb through shafts where suffocation was very possible. Once in the chimney, if they were frightened to go up, the master would light a fire under them or prick the soles of their feet.

Some efforts were made to better the conditions for the sweeps. A Bill in 1788 stopped boys under eight from being apprentices. The Act was almost totally ignored. The Society for Superseding the Necessity of Climbing Boys was formed about 1800. It tried to encourage the use of a special brush instead of small boys. An article in

8 A child sweep, underfed, and black with dust from crawling through the chimneys.

The Lady's Magazine, 1802, reported the struggle of one little sweep:

The dangerous practice of forcing little chimney sweeps to climb up a nich on the outside of St George's Church, Hanover Sq, still continues. A dirty brute was yesterday employed for near two hours in forcing a child, at the risk of his life, to climb up the place alluded to; sometimes by sending another lad to poke him up, by putting his head underneath him, and at others by pricking him with a pin fastened to the end of a stick. The poor child, in the struggle to keep himself from falling, had rubbed the skin from his knees and elbows, while the perspiration arising from fear and exertion covered his face and breast as if water had been thrown upon him.

At least one, Thomas Cooper, escaped a master sweep's clutches:

We were not half-way towards Lea, when we were met by Cammidge, a master Chimney-sweeper, and his two apprentices bending under huge soot bags. He began to entice my mother into an agreement for me to be his apprentice, and took out two golden guineas from his purse and offered them to her. She looked anxiously at them, but shook her head; and I clung trembling to her apron and cried, 'Oh, mammy, mammy, do not let the grimy man take me away'. 'No, my dear bairn, he shall not,' she answered and away we went — leaving the chimney-sweeper in a rage. (*The Life of Thomas Cooper*)

9 In the country, children worked with the adults in the fields. This four-wheeled drill plough, fitted with a seed and manure hopper, was invented in 1745. New efficient machinery paved the way for the agricultural revolution.

Other work

Children worked in other jobs as well, In the Midlands brickyards little girls each caught and threw 15 tons of bricks between 6 in the morning and 8 at night. In the eastern counties children of 5 to 16 were hired out to undertakers. The children worked weeding and cutting thistles. In some places children could be 'hired' from parish authorities and others for 4d a night. Beggars who hired children often mutilated them, to gain pity (and more coins) from the public.

In the country children worked with their parents in the fields from an early age.

Girls often worked as 'milk-maids' for dairymen. They wore white pinafores, black taffeta bonnets, and a yoke over their shoulders from which hung buckets. Milk-maids were expected to get up at 3 or 4 in the morning and start their working day by milking 10 or 12 cows. Many girls worked as servants in richer homes. Abandoned children or children who ran away to towns were often adopted by criminals. For them 'work' was picking pockets or prostitution.

10 A milk-maid carrying the heavy pails by means of a yoke.

3 Schools and Education

Every young person must go to school in Britain today, but that was not so in the eighteenth century. Schooling was disorganized and haphazard. The poor had less chance of schooling than the well-to-do, and girls had less opportunity than boys. There were, however, more and more schools as the century went on — of very different kinds.

Charity schools

Charity schools began in the early part of the century. These were for the boys and girls of the labouring poor. The main aim

11 A school in 1739. Children were treated harshly by their teachers; the sticks in the master's hand for whipping were used often.

12 A charity school.

was to teach children religion, and how to read and write. They also taught handcraft activities, such as cobbling shoes, printing, carpentry, knitting, sewing, spinning and straw-plaiting. Some efforts were made to sell what the children made to help support the schools. By 1740 there were nearly 2000 of these charity schools in England.

Lessons in the charity schools were by rote. The aim was to turn out good, reliable God-fearing workers. In summer the school day lasted from 5 or 6 in the morning until 8 or 9 at night, with short breaks for meals. (In the winter the day was from 6 or 7 in the morning until 7 or 8 at night). The

schools were voluntary, so no one had to go if they did not wish to. It was often difficult to attract pupils in the country areas, since parents preferred their children to work in the fields to help the family income.

Sunday Schools started in 1780 in Gloucester, and like the charity schools, they taught religion. They were mainly for children working in industry who could only go to school on Sunday. The hours were from 9 to 6 with breaks for dinner and divine service. The feeling was that even overworked children of the mills should be able to read. By 1833, six out of ten children in England were attending some sort of school and three of these were at Sunday School.

Public schools

Public schools, such as Eton (founded in 1440) and Harrow (founded in 1571), were originally for the sons of tradesmen and craftsmen. But gradually they attracted more and more boys from the upper classes. By the end of the eighteenth century, the main schools were largely for the sons of gentlemen. Conditions were hard in the public schools. Food was often very bad. Disorder, bullying, and general uproar was common. There were many riots. The 'fagging' system was a way in which the older boys held power over smaller boys.

13 'The departure for school'. The tearful boy leaving for boarding school is being handed a basket of fruit and another basket of food for the journey by his small sister.

The older boys forced the young boys to make their beds for them, supply them with ink and paper, and generally act as servants.

There was much whipping and caning at the public schools. One schoolmaster was so used to flogging that when he could find no reason for it he suggested that he should whip the boys in advance for their

14 A school in 1800. The boy standing on the stool wearing a 'dunce cap' is being punished for not knowing his lessons.

15 The grammar school at Harrow, Middlesex.

next mischief. Dr Samuel Parr of Harrow thought himself kindly because he never flogged a boy twice in the same lesson.

The rebellions at the public schools were as common as the floggings. In the Great Rebellion at Winchester in 1793 the rebels took the keys of the school and locked themselves in. At Rugby in 1797 the boys mined the headmaster's study with gunpowder and made a bonfire of their desks. The boys at Harrow set up a road block and blew up the governor's carriage. It is not surprising that parents who could afford it often kept their sons at home and hired a tutor.

Grammar schools

Grammar schools were originally for 'poor and deserving' boys — but these, like the public schools, attracted more boys from richer homes. Most grammar schools took in pupils as boarders if necessary. As the roads were so poor in country areas, travel to and from school each day would have been impossible for many.

Private schools

Small private schools and 'dissenting academies' also existed for those who were excluded from the other schools and universities because of their religious beliefs. They developed a more modern educational system and taught mainly commercial subjects for boys, such as navigation, surveying, and European languages. The fees in the 1780s for the more expensive schools were about £20 to £25 a year for full boarders (excluding washing). Schools in the north were cheaper than schools in the south. Children under ten were boarded more cheaply. A year's education of a son of Mr Bennet cost £31 7s 6d in 1755. Here is one of his half-yearly bills reproduced in the original style and spelling:

For a year's boarding and schooling due at Midsummer	£10.10.—
Coach downe	3.—
2 writing books and 1 slate	3. 6
Whole Duty of Man	3.—
Ceasar's Commentaries	6.—
Letters	1. 1
Cutting and Curling Hair	1.—
Ribbon & Worsted	3.—
Pens Ink & Paper	3.—
3 shirts mended	1. 6
Weekly allowance	9.—
Mending cloaths	8.—
Shoemakers bill	6. 2
Coach to London	3.—
Set of Merchants Accounts	10. 6
Dancing	1. 1.—
	£14.12. 9

Parents had to be attracted to schools. The schools advertised and competed with each other for customers. Schools 'showed off' by giving plays and musical evenings. Some schools offered a military education, others preparation for life as a merchant. There were no competitive games at school in the eighteenth century.

Education for girls
The education of girls was generally not thought to be important. What schools there were taught reading, writing, needlework, and playing the harpsichord. A large number of girls stayed at home and were taught by a governess. Mothers taught them about keeping a house and cooking meals. A writer in the *London Chronicle* in 1759 suggested that:

girls should be well instructed in all kinds of plain work, reading, writing, accounts, pastry, pickling, preserving, and other branches of cooking; be taught to weave and wash lace and other linen. Thus instructed they may be of great comfort and assistance to their parents and husbands; they may have a right to expect the kindliest treatment from their mistresses; they are to be respected as useful members of society; whereas young ladies are the most useless of God's creatures...

Lady Mary Wortley Montagu thought the value of book learning for girls was very doubtful, and that any girl with such learning should hide it as she would a lame leg. Towards the end of the eighteenth century, day and boarding schools for richer girls became more common. These schools taught mainly music, dancing, and how to be charming. Schools for middle class girls also mainly prepared them for home and marriage. Book learning was thought to lessen a girl's chances of finding a husband.

Universities
Universities were only for the aristocracy or gentry, and women were excluded altogether. A few terms' residence was thought necessary to finish the education of a gentleman. There was no need to attend lectures, and no examinations. It was not until 1800 that Oxford made real demands on those seeking a degree.

After, or instead of, going to university, it was fashionable for a young man from a wealthy family to go on the 'Grand Tour'. With his tutor, he visited Europe and saw the sights of France and Italy.

Education for working children

While the Charity Schools and the Sunday Schools did help the education of the poor, there were still many that had little real chance for schooling. The Industrial Revolution meant that many children spent their days working in factories and mines. The Health and Morals of Apprentices Act 1802 said that factory children should have instruction two hours each day. But this was not enforced until 1833. These children were often taught while sitting on the floor of a warehouse, by an old workman with a reading primer and a cane. Exhausted by work, the children could hardly stay awake.

16 A cobbler, John Pounds of Portsmouth, acted as a voluntary schoolmaster to his poor neighbours' children while he mended shoes.

4 Home Life

Cuddling children was frowned upon by much of the upper and middle classes. They thought it bad for children to show them too much affection. Lady Portarlington remarked to her sister that in Ireland children actually put their arms round their father's neck and kissed him! She thought such behaviour would be very vulgar in England.

The upper classes paid little attention to their children in their nursery days. Nannies looked after the young children, and were often quite harsh. Little children were shut in dark cupboards. Children were also frightened into being good by dummies dressed as ghosts. Nurses who wanted to keep children in bed while they went off at night used these terrifying methods. Susan Sibbald wrote of 'ghosts' she saw as a child:

> I remember when both the nursery maids at Fowey wished to leave the nursery one evening. . . we were silenced by hearing the most dismal groanings and scratchings outside the partition next the stairs. The door was thrown open, and oh! horrors, there came in a figure, tall and dressed in white, with fire coming out of its eyes, nose and mouth it seemed. We were almost thrown into convulsions, and were not well for days, but dared not tell. (*The Memoirs of Susan Sibbald 1783-1812*)

Rocking in a cradle was usual for babies. But often babies were rocked violently to put them in a daze. Clockwork cradles could be

17 A late eighteenth-century family here gathers round the hearth in the evening.

wound to rock for 43 minutes.

Large families were very common and childless couples were rare — but there was little attention to child care in the eighteenth century. It was only towards the end of the century that there was concern with the upbringing of children.

Just as it was not considered proper to show affection to children, so the gentleman of the eighteenth century thought it unmanly to openly show affection to his wife. Marriage was the subject of endless jokes and sneers. The average age for marriage in the early eighteenth century was about 27 for men and 25 for women — but this lowered as a result of the Industrial Revolution. Divorce was very costly and difficult, needing a Special Act of Parliament.

Girls had more freedom and more chance to meet men than later in Victorian times. But marriages were often arranged by parents. Many daughters were virtually sold into marriage as though they were property. Marriage and motherhood were taught to be the goal of nearly all females.

Housing

Housing varied greatly between the labouring poor and the rich, between town and country, between North and South, East and West. The cramped country cottage of the labouring poor was likely to have

mud walls mixed with straw, a beaten mud floor, paper or rags at the window. The upper classes had elegant houses, with servants to look after them. Overcrowding was a feature of the time. But then privacy was not valued then as it is today. People found greater warmth and safety in huddling together.

18 King George III with his wife and the ten royal children. Large families were very common in the eighteenth century.

19 A father amuses his children with a finger
shadow puppet of a rabbit on the wall. Without
radio or television in the home, families made
their own amusements.

20 A street scene in Cardiff in 1797, showing how the small houses were huddled together in the provincial towns, and the farm animals mingled with the people in a common hubbub. A small boy is helping to drive the pigs along.

21 A home in 1797 which was also a place of work. Cottage industries produced all sorts of goods.

The mud cottage was common in many parts of the country where brick was dear and local stone was not available. But however simple, the country family was often better off than the poor in the towns — especially London. The country family might be able to collect wood for fuel, and could have a garden to grow vegetables. A local well or stream often had a better water supply than that which people had in towns.

Lack of transport increased the overcrowding and bad housing conditions for poorer families in towns. It was necessary for people to live near their work. The heart of London was a dirty, unpleasant place in which to live. All towns were very insanitary, unhealthy places. Already closely packed houses would be divided again to pack in more people and earn more profit for the landlords. There were frequent fires, and the collapse of houses in poor repair was common. After the Great Fire of London in 1666, however, most buildings tended to be made of brick rather than wood, and this helped to make them safer than they had been in the previous century.

Most poorer families, in the country as well as in the towns, lived in only one room. In towns, the very poorest lived in cellars approached by steps from the street. These

22 The fireplace was the focus of the home. The hearth offered the only heating, and was also the place for cooking and boiling water.

28

were dark, damp places very likely to flood in wet weather. As well as being homes, these were places of business well-suited to the small cobbler or greengrocer. The poor who could not even afford a cellar slept in sheds or on the street. Land in London was usually held by some wealthy landowner. In each house a 'housekeeper' rented lodgings to others. The first floor was most desirable for a room, then the second floor. The ground floor and garret came next. Least desirable were the cellars, because they were prone to damp.

In contrast to the overcrowding of the poor were the houses of the upper classes.

23 A drawing of Harwood House by the architect James Gibbs (1682-1754). Gibbs was concerned with symmetry, grace and dignity in architecture; he was the designer of St Martin-in-the-Fields and St Mary-le-Strand in London.

Gentlemen, merchants, better-paid clergy, professional men lived in fine homes with plenty of servants to keep them in order. Early eighteenth-century houses (known as Early Georgian) were very much concerned with symmetry and proportion. In the

24 This Georgian house stands at Twickenham in its own grounds.

closing years of the century, the style became simpler. Great stately homes were built in the style known as Palladian. The grounds surrounding these great houses were as important as the buildings themselves.

The houses of middle-class gentry often contained a hall, one or two dining rooms, and seven or eight bedrooms, a study, music room, or library. Farmhouses were more modest, with a dining room, bedroom and drawing room on the ground floor and a few bedrooms upstairs.

A window tax first started in the seventeenth century was made more widespread in the eighteenth. Every house with more than seven windows had to pay a tax. Most householders understandably had as few as possible, and instances where windows were bricked up to avoid paying the tax can still be seen in Georgian houses today. For lighting, cottagers gathered reeds and soaked them in coarse fat to make rush-lights. Candles lit the houses of the middle and upper classes.

Furniture

Beds were solid, with curtains and canopies, piles of blankets and pillows. Every year these beds would be taken to pieces and washed in vinegar and water. Bed bugs were still plentiful. Mattresses were stuffed with feathers. Children and servants usually slept on low wooden bedsteads without curtains.

31

32

26 The Octagon Room at Orleans House, Twickenham, was designed by James Gibbs. The walls are lavishly decorated with mock columns and statuary.

A chamber pot beneath the bed served as a toilet, as there was no proper sanitation. (In poor cottages children usually slept on a flock mattress directly on the ground.)

Baths, like water closets, were only for the rich until well into the nineteenth century. Bath-tubs were placed before the bedroom fire and filled with water carried upstairs by servants. Most people lived in cottages where the well or spring was some distance away, or in tenements where the water was fetched from a communal tap in the street. They were likely to agree with a Sussex grocer in the 1750s who felt a bath should be taken every spring.

Styles of furniture before Georgian times were called after the reigning monarchs (Elizabethan, Jacobean, Queen Anne, etc.). But from 1714 such styles were named after their designers, e.g. Chippendale, Hepplewhite, Sheraton. Mahogany wood imported from the West Indies became popular for good furniture. The furniture of the poor was generally just a bench, one or two chairs, a table and a bed.

By the beginning of the eighteenth century carpets were part of the furnishings of the well-to-do. Many of these were from Turkey and Persia. Poor people still strewed floors with sand or rushes.

27 A Hepplewhite sideboard, in the slim, elegant Georgian style.

Food

White bread and tea were a luxury in the eighteenth century. They were only for the well-to-do; labourers and their families ate brown bread, and drank ale or water. While some luxuries then have become commonplace today, other dishes familiar to eighteenth century children have disappeared from today's tables: 'Hasty Pudding' was a mixture of flour, water, brown sugar and butter; 'Bean Tansy' consisted of beans mixed with butter, eggs, pepper, salt, cloves, bacon and juice of the tansy; 'Crowdie' was broth thickened with oatmeal.

Both the town labourer's family and the farm labourer's family lived mainly on bread and cheese, with meat perhaps once a week. About half the labourer's income might be spent on bread alone. In the South, the brown bread was made of wheat. But in much of the North and West it was more commonly made of barley, rye, and oats. Home-baking of bread (and home-brewing of beer) was common practice in the early eighteenth century. Bakers first appeared in the villages of southern England in the middle of the eighteenth century. By the end of the century, many labouring families were fireless as fuel became scarcer. The cost of coal was too high for many. By 1815, regular home brewing of beer by the cottager had ceased over most of the country. In some ways the Northern diet was more varied than that of the South. More potatoes and more meat were eaten in the North; more families were able to keep a pig, and milk was more available.

The growth of towns had an important effect on what people ate. People bought more food and produced less themselves. In London the lack of cooking facilities in one-room lodgings led to a dependence on cook shops and sellers of pies. Many town wives worked in factories or in domestic service, which left them little time or energy for cooking anyway. Bought bread, potatoes boiled or roasted in their jackets, and bacon

which could be quickly fried became the common town food. Many people, not only in towns, went very short of food when harvests were bad and prices rose.

Children in factories provided their own food which they ate during breaks. But some pauper children who worked as near-slaves for mill owners were fed by the owners on an unappealing porridge seasoned with beef and pork brine. These half-starved children would go after pig's food.

While many poor families scarcely had enough, the well-to-do often ate more than was good for them. In the early part of the century the rich ate a large late breakfast, light cold lunch and early dinner about 5 or 6 pm. Breakfast often included cold roast beef, cheese and ale, fish, eggs, chops and steaks.

The English dinner was originally a midday meal but over the century it became common to dine later and later. By the end of the century, dinner was eaten late in London — but people still dined mid-day in the country and mid-afternoon in the towns. One woman's diary of 1779 recorded a meal with the Rector of Aston:

. . At 3:00 we sat down to table, which was covered with salmon at top, fennel sauce to it, melted butter, lemon pickle and soy; at the bottom a loin of veal roasted, on the one side kidney beans, on the other peas, and in the middle a hot pidgeon pie with yolks of egg in it. To the kidney beans and peas succeeded ham and chicken, and when everything was removed came a currant tart. . . After dinner we had water to wash, and when the cloth was taken away, gooseberries, currants and melon, wines and cyder.

35

29 The children of a wealthy family sample grapes from a street stall.

Well-to-do children did not eat quite such fancy menus as their parents, but they did eat the same kind of food. A letter from a young man to his father in 1735 reported:

Dear Papa,
We had a very good dinner, for we had at the first course three macerell, then after that we had beans and bacon and boyl'd chickens, and then we had four little plates pidgeons one rabbits, in an other gooseberry tart and sparrow grase and no desart. . .

Paris Cher Monſ.ʳ Trolaria

30 Two boys serve coffee to the customers in a Georgian coffee house. They are wearing wigs, and use aprons to protect their clothes.

Old recipes of the time seem quite amazing today. Queen of Scots soup was made of six chickens and eight eggs. Mrs Glass records six pounds of butter as enough for the crust of a goose pie. A quart of cream and whites of nine eggs are two ingredients of 'almond cream'. Uxbridge cake required a pound of wheat flour, seven pounds of currants, and four pounds of butter.

Coffee was a fashionable drink in Georgian times, and gentlemen would go to coffee houses in the towns to talk business and see their friends. Children did not go to coffee houses, but young boys would work in them, serving the coffee to the customers.

Clothing

In the early 1700s richer children often wore a 'pudding' or padded cap. They also often wore 'leading strings'. These were two wide ribbons sewn to the robe behind each shoulder and hanging down at the back. It was only since the seventeenth century that a special way of dressing for children began. While poor children continued to dress much as their parents, there were some special items of clothing for middle and upper class children.

Boys and girls were dressed alike (in long petticoats) until they were four or five years old. Then boys were 'breeched' and

31 Benjamin Hallet (a *boy aged under five*) playing
a public concert in Drury Lane in 1748. Boys were
commonly dressed in feminine clothes until the age
of four or five, then put straight into grown-up
breeches. This fashion continued until the late
1770s.

32 *The Graham Children* by Hogarth (1742) shows girls wearing full skirts and lace bodices. The boy wears a waisted coat with large cuffs; on his knee is a box organ.

thereafter dressed much as their fathers — with a coat, waistcoat, and breeches. In the 1780s boys began to wear trousers (which were not the fashion for men until the nineteenth century). Small boys in the 1790s wore a 'skeleton suit', which had a short tight-fitting jacket. Boys wore their hair quite long, to the shoulders, until the end of the century, when short hair became more correct. Boys also sometimes wore long wigs, like their fathers.

33 It was a tug-of-war to make the lady fit the
fashion! Black servant boys (as shown in the picture)
were also fashionable at the time. Africans had been
brought to work in England from about the year
1550.

Girls dressed much like their mothers, with long skirts touching the ground. Some girls even wore stiff hoop petticoats. Long or short cloaks were generally worn outdoors. Hats and bonnets were very popular. In the 1740s to the 1760s these hats were usually quite flat, but from the 1770s these were often quite high. White linen caps were worn indoors.

Wigs for adults and children were popular for much of the eighteenth century. A tax on hair powder in 1795 helped to end what must have been a very difficult fashion. But like most fashions, it had its funny side. One little girl in the eighteenth century sat in church watching a mouse popping in and out of the headress on the lady in front. (In fact, silver wire nightcaps were sold to go over these hairstyles 'so strong no mouse or rat could gnaw through them'.)

Ordinary working adults — and their children — wore much simpler clothes, often secondhand. The introduction of cheap, washable cotton cloth by the end of the century did much to improve the clothing of the working poor. The gowns and petticoats, knee-breeches and long coats worn by ordinary people were quite plain. Farm workers wore coarse linen and woollen smocks. The rags worn by the very poor were quite horrible. Their one set of clothes might be sewn round them, or tied by string. They often went barefoot or tied straw round their feet and legs to keep out the cold.

While the fancy fashions of the day were really only for the well-to-do, poorer people liked to copy these when they could. At one charity school for girls the uniform was short cropped hair, plain dresses, long mittens, white aprons, and mob caps. One bold girl powdered her hair and face with flour. The teachers were very cross. She was 'instantly stripped, birched, and scrubbed before the whole school'.

At the end of the eighteenth century, fashion became somewhat simpler and more practical. Tight bodices and hoops were discarded. Wigs and powder disappeared. Well-to-do men and women — and their children — wore less fancy clothes. There was a better understanding of children's needs, and therefore less physical restraint in their clothes. Girls had more simple flowing dresses from the 1780s on, with large floppy hats for outdoor wear. Boys' trousers became loose slacks, with slits at the ankle for more freedom.

34   By 1799 dress for adults and children had become simpler and more comfortable.

5 Health

In 1700, the population of England and Wales was five million. By 1750 the total was six million, and by 1800 it was ten million. Nearly half the population lived in towns and worked in the factories. This 'population explosion' was due to the slightly better conditions in which people lived at the end of the century. Somewhat more children were living to become adults, and more adults were living longer.

However, no one really understood the importance of hygiene. Many children died from illness and disease because their parents and doctors did not know what caused it or how to cure it. In 1762 54 per cent of children died before they were two years old, 69 per cent were dead before they were five. More people died in childhood than at any other time. Even by the early 1800s almost one-half of the children born in Britain died by the age of twelve.

Thrush is just one of many infectious diseases common in the eighteenth century but hardly ever seen in Britain today. The disease is a fungus over the mouth and tongue of infants, caused by poor food and lack of cleanliness. A mouthwash including ether, white wine and honey was the treatment. Smallpox, convulsions, and rickets were other main health problems.

Baby care

Birth itself was very dangerous in the eighteenth century. Often either the mother or child died — and sometimes both. Many men who lost wives in childbirth married two or three times.

'Swaddling' was one practice which was probably harmful to babies. 'Swaddling' meant tying the infant in a bandage so it looked rather like a parcel. They believed that babies would hurt themselves if left to move their limbs about, and swaddled babies were much easier to care for. They could be hung on a peg on the wall or put in any corner. Swaddled infants cried less, slept more, their hearts slowed down, and they were generally withdrawn. Swaddled babies simply needed less attention. There is some suggestion that babies in the eighteenth century began walking, on average, a few months later than babies today partly because of the effects of swaddling. By the end of the eighteenth century in England, swaddling was on the way out.

Another practice which was on the way out was wet-nursing. A wet-nurse is a woman who breastfeeds other women's children for them. During the eighteenth century, more women began breastfeeding their own babies. Those who did not often used a substitute called 'pap' (a mixture of bread, water, milk, and brown sugar). One famous doctor, George Armstrong, wrote in his *Essay on the Diseases Most Fatal to Infants* (1771):

I do not advise the dry nursing of infants when they can be properly suckled, yet I would not have parents to be discour-

43

aged from trying it when it becomes requisite. There are two ways of feeding children who are bred up by the hand;

the one is by means of a horn, and the other is with a boat or spoon. The latter is preferable.

The first exercise I shall mention proper for infants, is dandling, which is certainly of service to divert them, and keep them awake; but then it should be done very gently for a good while at

35 This page of instruction for midwives delivering babies shows the tools used, and how to deliver a baby using forceps. Birth was a very risky time for both mother and baby.

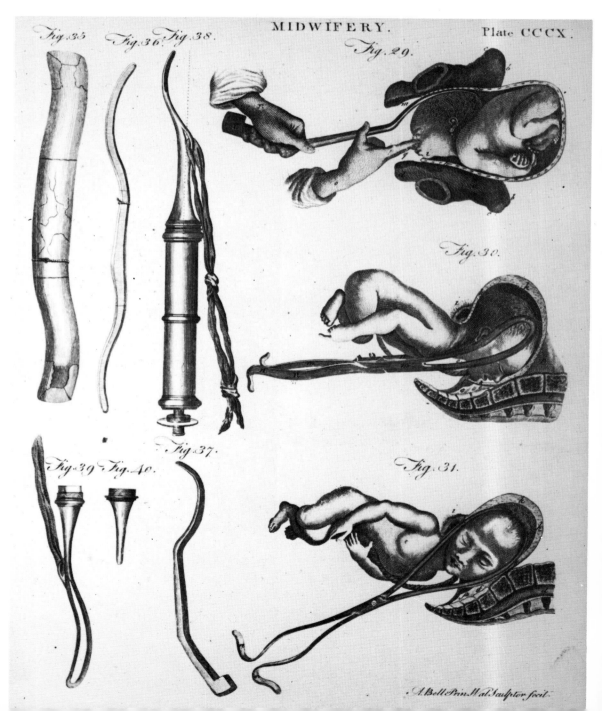

MIDWIFERY.   Plate CCCX.

first, and never with a jerk. Neither should they be hoisted up high in the air between the hands, as some people heedlessly do; for they begin very early to be susceptible of fear, much sooner than persons not accustomed to them would imagine. But the most useful exercise for very young infants, is rubbing with the hand; which cannot be too often repeated, nor continued too long at a time. They should be well rubbed all over before the fire, twice a day at least, that is, morning and evening, when they are dressed and undressed.

A doctor of the early 1800s, William Buchan, wrote in *Domestic Medicine* also giving advice on children's health. He suggested the simplest diet for infants, protesting against the sugar which Dr Armstrong thought useful:

It is strange how people come to think that the first thing given to a child should be drugs. Midwives never fail to give syrups, oils, etc. whether they be necessary or not. Few things prove more hurtful to infants than the common method of sweetening their food. It entices them to take more than they ought to do, which makes them grow fat and bloated. All strong liquors are hurtful to children. Some parents teach their children to guzzle ale, and other fermented liquors. Such a practice cannot fail to do mischief. Milk, water, butter milk, or whey, are the most proper for children to drink. If they have anything stronger, it may be fine small beer, or a little wine mixed with water.

Sugar was also added to medicines to make them less nasty to children. Robert Thornton MD, among others, suggested adding honey, sugar, treacle, or molasses to 'horrid medicines' — instead of suddenly appearing from behind a curtain with a whip! Strong drugs such as opium were much used for children as well as adults. Gin was given to children as a sedative, as was laudanum (an alcoholic tincture of opium). George Young MD, in *A Treatise on Opium* wrote:

The weaning-illness of infants is often attended with a diarrhoea, which is probably owing to their change of diet from breast-milk to spoon-meat: the best way of preventing it is to accustom the children for some months before their weaning, to such diet as differs least from breast-milk, and to wean them gradually. But if notwithstanding a looseness comes on, four or five drops of liquid laudanum, with the absorbent powders, given every night in any convenient form, will seldom fail, unless after eating too much; for an opiate always disagrees with a plentiful meal.

Medical knowledge
Besides drugs, people turned to herbal cures. There was usually a 'wise woman' in the locality who collected plants from the countryside, and made charms and amulets. A pine cone averted the evil eye. Amber was said to keep children from danger. A necklace of orris root hung round a baby's neck was said to prevent convulsions. One woman's cure for fever was a spider shut in a goose quill, well-sealed, and hung about the child's neck as low as the stomach.

Some standard treatments were used by doctors. Phlebotomy, or bleeding, was common whereby leeches were applied to the patient's limbs, or his veins were cut then bound up again. A clyster, or enema, was also often used. A blister put on various parts of the body was thought a useful way of draining 'evil' humours from the infected area. Cupping was used to remove pressure.

Smallpox was one of the most widespread diseases of the eighteenth century. About one person in thirteen in every generation was killed by it until Edward Jenner discovered that inoculation with cowpox prevented smallpox, and his vaccine gained general acceptance in 1801. In London, about 60 out of every 100 people caught smallpox and 20 of those died. Those who recovered were often disfigured. One Thomas Cooper recalls having the disease as a child:

> My earliest recollections of Gainsborough begin with my taking the small-pox, which I had so severely that I was blind for nineteen days, was worn til the bones came through my skin, at the knees, hips, and elbows, and was thrice believed to be dead. Measles and scarlet fever came close upon my weak recovery from the more fell disease. (*The Life of Thomas Cooper*)

Diseases like smallpox, typhoid, typhus, and dysentery spread rapidly in the eighteenth century — especially in slum districts.

36 'The First Vaccination' shows Edward Jenner inoculating an eight year old boy in 1796. Jenner's vaccine was a breakthrough in fighting the dreaded smallpox.

Undernourished people in overcrowded, poor housing were ready victims. A working class family in London often lived in a single room, with one bed sleeping from three to eight people. Sheets, if any, were changed at most three times a year. The room would be crammed with bits of furniture and the tools and materials used by the father and mother in their trade. It was impossible to sweep or dust. Cracks in the doors and walls would be stuffed with rags, and there would be a heavy smell from an open drain. As living conditions improved, these diseases were brought more under control.

There was no running tap water in Georgian times. All household water was from rainwater kept in cisterns, or else transported to the house from wells in casks. It was hard to get pure drinking water. Few adults drank water without adding wine, spirits or ale. Only very young children were likely to drink water on its own. They therefore fell victim to water-borne germs from dysentery to typhus.

As water was not easily obtained, people did not bathe often. Clothes were washed only once a month at most. The general

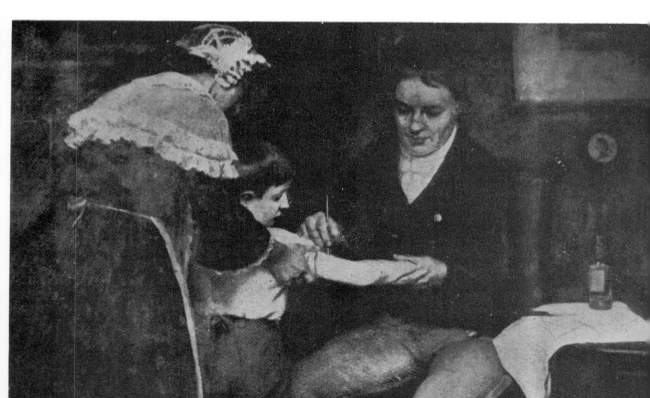

dirt and filth of towns, and of London in particular, did much to help the spread of disease. Refuse from houses was thrown on to the streets. There was no proper drainage system.

Hospitals

At the beginning of Georgian times, medical knowledge was very low. There was no understanding that dirt helped to spread disease. There were several hospitals, but their conditions were bad, and they probably did more harm than good. There were no anaesthetics and few antiseptics. As the century went on, standards rose, but there were no children's hospitals in the eighteenth century, nor were children allowed into general hospitals.

Children suffered the general health problems of the time, but they also suffered from being abandoned and neglected. Unwanted babies were just left in the streets to die. Homeless children wandered in towns. Many deserted children died of starvation and exposure.

Thomas Coram (1668-1751), a retired sea captain, was moved by the sight of babies left in the streets of London. He managed to open a Foundling Hospital where unwanted infants could be brought. A Royal Charter for the incorporation of the Hospital was granted in 1739. The doors opened in March of 1741 and the response was overwhelming. Crowds of women rushed in with babies in their arms. The hospital was full within four hours. Most of the children had been drugged to keep them quiet.

Within a few years the Foundling Hospital had done such good work that it was given a grant to take in children from the country as well as London. This was a disaster. An ever-growing number of children were dumped, often more dead than alive, into the basket at its doors. The hospital could hardly cope.

While some of the children were delivered clean and well-dressed, others were ill and ragged. An early rule of the hospital was that people leaving children should 'affix on them some particular writing or other distinguishing mark or token'. An early note read: 'A female child, aged about 6 weeks, with a blue figured ribbon, and purple and white printed linen sleeves, turned up with red and white.'

Deserted infants were sometimes raised by the parish authorities who sent them to work at mills and elsewhere at an early age. In some cases, children were abandoned in a most unusual way:

London, March, 1803. A few days ago, a woman presented, at a pawn-broker's office, a bundle of clothes as a pledge, demanding at the same time to be informed of the sum which the pawn-broker would lend. . . she was answered that eighteen shillings was the highest sum that could be advanced on the goods; but, as the woman seemed to consider the sum to be inadequate to her wants, she repacked her bundle with great care, in the presence of the clerk, and withdrew to the door. In about a few seconds she returned, and said she had changed her mind and would accept the sum offered her, laying, at the same time, a bundle on the counter: she accordingly, received the money, and went away. The clerk took up the bundle to convey it upstairs to the store-room, and had proceeded a part of the way, when he perceived something to move within the bundle; and, upon opening the outside folds of the bundle, his astonishment upon perceiving a fine boy may be easier conceived than expressed. It should be stated that the pawn-broker, having had the child christened, and called Bundle-boy, provided it with proper clothes and a nurse, and has exercised the most attentive humanity to the little orphan. (*The Lady's Magazine*, Vol. XXXIII)

6 Religion

During the eighteenth century the state religion was that of the Church of England. Protestantism had replaced Roman Catholicism (during the Reformation of the Church) in the sixteenth century, and thereafter the monarch was the official Head of the Church instead of the Pope. For a long time Protestants and Roman Catholics had persecuted

each other, and each had sent many martyrs to the stake; but by the eighteenth century a belief in religious toleration had spread through Britain, and small religious sects were allowed to flourish.

John (1703-91) and Charles (1707-88) Wesley began the movement called Methodism, which encouraged the congregation to join in the church services. A child going to a Methodist church would enjoy singing the stirring marching hymns which the Wesley brothers had composed.

The Quakers (founded by George Fox in 1652) were another religious sect which had a small, strong following during the eighteenth century. They set themselves high standards of morals and discipline. A child born into a Quaker family would have a strict and solemn upbringing, and would be expected to wear dark coloured clothes at all times. He would also have to attend the long religious services in silence. Elizabeth Fry (1778-1845), who was a pioneer in prison reform, was a Quaker.

However, most families belonged to the Church of England, and children were expected to go to church at least once every Sunday. The churches were very cold, and sometimes rushes or straw were laid on the floor to make them warmer. Large wooden pews were placed at the front of the church for rich families, while poor people sat at the back on hard seats. Some pews belonging to the rich had tables and fireplaces, and the best pews were usually rented to wealthy families.

Early in the century, Sunday was a day for church, and all shops had to be closed; but by the end of the century many shops opened on Sunday, and the day was often spent on amusements rather than prayer. In some areas little interest was shown in churches, and they were allowed to fall into bad repair. In country areas, however, the church was important to people's lives, and the great events such as baptism, marriage and death were all important religious ceremonies. Each family's Prayer Book contained the family records, with the dates of births and deaths and the family tree.

Superstition played a great part in religion, and there were many superstitions about children. No infant was to be taken out until it went to be christened. A baby's right hand was not to be washed, so that it should gather riches throughout its life. A baby's nails must not be cut for a year for fear the child would grow up 'light fingered'. If a baby went into a strange house, its mouth was to be filled with salt. A piece of coral hung round the neck was good protection against evil spirits and bad luck.

For working children in the factories and towns, Sunday was their only day of rest, but many of them still went to Sunday school (their only form of education) and attended church.

37 Going to church was a social as well as religious occasion. A wealthy landlord, Sir Roger de Coverley, goes to church, surrounded by his tenants.

7 Crime and Punishment

A boy of ten was hanged for stealing a penknife. A girl of fourteen was hanged for taking a handkerchief. Nearly 200 crimes were punishable by hanging in the eighteenth century — including picking a pocket to the value of a shilling, and damaging Westminster Bridge. Children were as harshly dealt with in public as adults, and were often roughly punished at home and school. Children were taken along to public executions, which were a grand amusement to the crowds. It was the custom to whip children after these executions — probably because their parents became so excited. This began to fade by 1765.

Many people writing about their childhood in the eighteenth century mentioned the punishments they were given. Mrs Sherwood remembered having to translate fifty lines of Virgil a day while imprisoned in the stocks. Charlotte Clarke wrote about being tied to a table leg. Fanny Kemble accounted a week's imprisonment in a tool shed. Heavy thrashing for boys was expected. A sad tale was told of a girl of three in the early nineteenth century. Her father's special punishment was to order her to the lowest step of the stair. She was not to move until permission was given. One night her father forgot her. When the footman brought wine and water up at midnight he found the poor little girl lying there asleep.

While treatment of children in the eighteenth century seems harsh, it must be remembered that life itself was rough. Robberies and assault were frequent — and there was no organized police force in London until 1829. By the early nineteenth century, a changing attitude was taking place. Some old penalties were being abolished (the stocks in 1826, pillory in 1837, public whipping of women in 1819). This softening attitude had an effect on how children were treated as well. The story of Patrick M'Donald in *The Complete Newgate Calendar* in the early nineteenth century shows that understanding was sometimes shown:

The miserable object of the present case, an emaciated lad of about fourteen, appeared at the bar at the Old Bailey. He was indicted for stealing a jacket, being almost naked, valued at fourteen shillings. Being asked what he had to say in his defence, he told an affecting tale that he was a cabin-boy in a merchant vessel which arrived six months before, but returned without him; that he found himself destitute; and that cold and hunger alone had compelled him to steal clothes and food.

One of the jury asked him if he had eaten anything that day, to which he answered 'No, sir; nor a bit the day before.' He then burst into tears, which produced such an effect that the sheriff gave him some silver, and the jury, before they gave their verdict, each handed him a shilling.

The judge then ordered that the boy should be taken care of, and observed that he would then procure his pardon.

38 A mother teaches her child scripture history from the paintings on the Dutch tiles surrounding the fireplace.

While this child of poverty and wretchedness was withdrawing, shillings, from all parts of the court and gallery, were thrown to him, which amount to a sum sufficient to clothe and nourish him.

39 A public hanging was greatly enjoyed by the spectators.

40 Children look on, as people jeer and throw rotten fruit at the four men in the pillory.

41 As the women argue, a boy furtively steals
fruit from one basket, while a dog makes away
with a fish from the other. On the left, a gentleman
is alighting from a sedan chair.

53

8 Travel and Transport

Most children travelled very little in the early eighteenth century. Roads linking towns were often mere tracks. Travel was difficult. Goods went by pack-horses, river or sea. People went mostly on horseback or on foot. But there was very much improvement of transport and roads over the century. Until the 1750s, roads were very poor. They were uncomfortable in dry weather and often impassable when it rained. Pack-horses, sometimes more than one hundred in a line, were the easiest way to transport goods on land. Wheeled vehicles had a difficult time as the ruts, mud and pot-holes on the roads were so bad.

The stage coaches of the early eighteenth century were heavy vehicles covered with dull black leather and studded with nails. The window frames and wheels were painted red, and the windows were often covered with leather curtains. The roof of the coach was rounded. The coachman and guard sat on an outside seat. These coaches did not average more than 25 miles a day.

Poor people, when they travelled (which was not often) either walked or went in a stage-waggon. The waggon was a long vehicle covered by a hood, drawn by a team of eight cart-horses. The waggons travelled slowly, about two miles an hour. While very uncomfortable, these waggons were safer than coaches as highwaymen never stopped them.

The poor roads prevented farming from becoming progressive. Farmers produced only enough for local needs, as it was so difficult to transport goods to markets.

The main reason for the bad roads was the lack of a road authority. The job of keeping up the roads fell on each parish through which the road passed. Each parishioner was required by law to work unpaid six days a year on the roads in his parish. But the work was often neglected.

There was much improvement of roads between the 1750s and the 1780s as the turnpike trusts were revived. The turnpike system first started in the reign of Charles II (1660-1685). Money was raised for the upkeep of highways by levying tolls with bars or pikes placed across roads. In the eighteenth-century system, toll-gates took the place of the old turnpikes. At each gate a toll-house was built for the pikeman who collected tolls. People were much against the new toll-gates at first, mainly because they wanted better roads but did not want to pay for them. But gradually public opinion was won over. Charles Dickens, the novelist, described the irritating delays at toll-gates, especially at night:

The stopping at the turnpike where the man was gone to bed, and knocking at the door until he answered with a smothered shout from under the bedclothes in the little room above, where the faint light was burning and presently came down, nightcapped and shivering, to throw the gate wide open . . .

Wheeled transport became much more common on English roads once the turn-

42 A stage-waggon. The driver rides alongside rather than on top.

pike trusts began their work. But still many children lived in small country towns and villages that could not be reached by any sort of vehicle. By the 1830s the main roads became safer and better. Hills were flattened and valleys filled in. Roads were given all-weather surfaces.

When the aristocracy or gentry travelled they had the choice of their own carriage drawn by their own horses, travelling 'post', or the mail or stage coaches. Travelling 'post' meant either hiring horses from stage to stage to draw the carriage, or hiring post-chaises and horses from stage to stage. A post-chaise was a small closed carriage built to carry two passengers. Changing at every stage meant moving baggage from one chaise to another.

It was in the middle years of the century that the stage-coaches running regularly between fixed stages (usually inns) appeared. These took two days from London to Bristol, and ten to twelve days from London to Edinburgh. These made travelling for the middle classes somewhat easier.

In 1784 mail coaches came into being. These were much better than the stage-

43 A stage-coach on the busy Newmarket Road. The growth of inns encouraged more travel — just as more travelling encouraged the growth of inns.

coaches and were popular with travellers. These charged twice as much as ordinary coaches, but were twice as fast. Until these mail coaches, post boys (usually on horses) carried the mails. They changed horses at inns called post-houses. They also hired out horses to the public.

Good inns were very rare until travelling became easier in the early nineteenth century. The improved stage-coaches of the early nineteenth century attracted more passengers. These passengers needed to be fed and lodged. In the early eighteenth

century the inns were very rough indeed. The artist Hogarth and some friends put up at an inn in Kent in 1732. The five of them could only get three beds between them. The sheets were so damp that they had to sleep in their clothes. They woke to find their eyes and hands swollen with gnat bites. One found a small boy asleep in his bed. It was the custom to write on the windows when staying at an inn. Some people carried diamond-point pencils for this purpose. Names, verses and sayings covered the windows of a popular inn.

The improvements in road transport helped the movement of goods as well as people. But heavy goods still needed to be moved on water. Growing industries needed coal from the coalfields. This prompted much building of inland waterways. The Duke of Bridgewater's Canal built by James Brindley, and opened in 1761, began it all. During 1770-94 Parliament authorized the building of 81 canals. Often these canals were easier to build than roads. The canals were useful for carrying bulky goods such as coal, corn and pottery — but not fresh foods. There were never many passengers on the canals — but poor children were sometimes sent by barge to work in cotton mills. A whole way of life grew up on the canal, and a child born into a family who lived on a barge would be expected to help in the work at an early age.

It was the need for something better than canals that led industry to finance railway development. The first steam locomotive built solely for the rails operated in Cornwall in 1804. By the 1830s there were no more than 400 miles of railway working in Britain. Most were in the North, mainly to carry coal.

Travel within London was mainly by hackney coach. Tradesmen did not like these because they claimed passengers could not look at shop windows. By 1771 there were thousands of these on London streets. At first these were heavy noisy vehicles. Iron shutters over the windows allowed passengers to look out without being seen. Later the shutters were removed and the windows were glazed. Sedan chairs were also used in London, mainly by fashionable people. The carriers were known to set a lady down in the middle of the street and demand double pay before they would lift her again.

Besides the hackney coaches and sedan chairs, it was possible to hire a waterman and be rowed. This was used by people

44 Children sit with the adults in the inn as they drink ale and smoke their long clay pipes. A dog is enclosed in a treadmill to drive the roasting spit below.

45 A demonstration of an early locomotive pulling an open-topped carriage. (Taken from a watercolour drawing by T.P. Rowlandson.)

living near the river. The streets were generally bad for traffic and in rainly weather they were almost impassable. Children had no raised pavements to walk on until the 1820s, so walking or travelling in winter cannot have been very pleasant.

46 A hackney-cab in 1790.

9 Entertainments

Sports

'The English beat cockerels to death with clubs, and throw dead dogs and cats at one another on certain festival days.' These pastimes were reported by one shocked French visitor to Britain in the early 1700s. He was also distressed by football:

> In cold weather you sometimes see a score of rascals in the streets kicking at a ball, and they will break panes of glass and smash the windows of coaches and also knock you down without the slightest compunction; on the contrary, they will roar with laughter.

47 A boy stands in the viewing gallery of the cock-fight. Children were commonly taken to see brutal gambling sports. If a man made a losing bet he could not pay, he was put in a basket and dangled over the ring.

Gambling was the favourite pastime of the century, for all classes. Anything might be the excuse for a bet, for children as well as adults. Some gentlemen seeing a passerby fall down on the pavement promptly laid a bet on whether or not he was dead. (Those who said he was, strongly objected to attempts to help him.) Violent, cruel sports with a chance to bet were very popular. Cock-fighting, hare-hunting, and bear- and bull-baiting were enthusiastically followed. De la Rochfoucauld has described a cockfight:

They have a large round table covered with a carpet, and two cocks of a particular breed with a lust for battle are set upon it. Their wings and tails are clipped; their beaks are filed down a little and to each of their legs a strong steel spur is firmly fixed. This is the weapon with which they fight. The spectators make enormous bets and have the keenest interest in the cock on which they have put their money. After they have fought a number of rounds and have freely used their spurs, it nearly always happens that both cocks are almost equally exhausted and both covered with blood. At length one of them, with supreme effort, overpowers and kills his adversary. The whole fight sometimes lasts three or four hours. All fighting cocks have names that are known throughout the country. . . Sometimes the victor dies soon after his defeated rival.

48 Cricket was very popular in the eighteenth century.

49 A boy of thirteen enjoys fishing.

Bull-baiting was just as brutal. In some places it took place almost every Sunday. The bull was tied by a fairly long rope to a stake and dogs were loosed at him one by one. Sometimes the bull's horns were blunted so the dog would be tossed rather than gored. A dog tossed high would be likely to break his back in a fall. The bulldog was specially bred for this sport. Sometimes the bull not only killed some of the dogs but also broke loose and hurt spectators. The bull was not only attacked by dogs but pricked with sharp stones or surrounded by

50 Children in the late eighteenth century playing with snowballs.

burning straw. Liverpool had an annual bull-baiting festival.

Even cricket (for which the rules were laid down in 1744) had its rough side, as spectators brawled after the games. Boxing and fist-fights generally were very popular. Courage, or 'bottom' as it was called, was important — and children were as quick as anyone to prove they had 'bottom'. Children also enjoyed quieter sports, such as fishing, flying kites, and swimming in summer, and skating and tobogganing in winter.

However, both children and adults loved to watch suffering and torture. Crowds would gather in holiday spirit to watch hangings at Tyburn, or to tease inmates at a lunatic asylum. On one occasion a boy was half-hanged then cut down and whipped through the town as a warning to him against begging.

Festivals

Fairs and carnivals at towns and villages were also popular mass amusements. Bartholomew Fair took place for several weeks in London every summer. There were many stalls and booths, selling goods, showing freaks and tricksters of every kind. In the year 1788-9 the River Thames froze from the end of November for seven weeks. A Frost Fair was held on the river, with puppet shows, giants and dwarfs, and stalls for gingerbread. Oxen were roasted whole and slices of meat were sold.

There were of course special holidays with their own celebrations. Guy Fawkes Day celebrated the capture and execution

51 The crowds and entertainers at the Edmonton Statute Fair. A girl, holding her doll, and a boy, carrying a toy barrow, hold on to their mother. Behind them a dancing bear is sampling the goods on a gingerbread stall.

of Guy Fawkes in 1606, when he had attempted to blow up the Houses of Parliament. Boys collected fuel for huge bonfires and made 'Guys' which were stuffed with straw and dressed in old clothes. These were often very large figures, and were taken through the streets accompanied by torchlight procession, with supporters shouting and singing.

Christmas was celebrated with much feasting and merriment in some parts of Britain, but not in London. The shops in London were closed, but otherwise Christmas was hardly noticed. New Year's Day was little regarded in the eighteenth century.

52 March Fair at Brough, Westmorland, was a typical country fair with side shows and musicians. Coal and cattle were on sale, and cake booths were run by women called 'spice wives'.

On St Valentine's Day it was sometimes the custom that the first girl whom a young man saw on that morning (who was not in his own family) was his Valentine. Usually a boy would send a present to a girl of his choice (a handkerchief, ribbons, or gloves). Later in the century the Valentine card was sold in stationer shops and became quite popular.

On Good Friday, boys came round the

streets very early selling hot cross buns. Easter eggs were given as presents on Easter Sunday.

Oak Apple Day on 29th May was celebrated with much festivity, to commemorate the restoration of Charles II to the throne in 1660 (he had hidden in an oak tree to avoid being captured after the battle of Worcester in 1651). Green boughs were collected from the country. Every house had an oak tree with golden oak apples or gilded balls to represent oak apples. There were streamers of flowers and flags across streets. Small boys and youths formed processions. Everyone had to wear an oak apple or at least a bunch of oak leaves.

53 *The Penny Wedding* by D Allan (1795).
Country dances and celebrations were held in large barns; the children are watching from the hay loft.

54 An engraving of children in the late eighteenth century playing marbles.

Games

'Marbles', 'Hunt the Slipper' and 'Blind Man's Bluff' were favourite children's games. 'Bear-Leader' was a game for several children. One would be blind-folded and lead another child on his hands and knees with a cord. It was the job of the blind-folded child to protect the 'bear', crouched beside him, from the other children. A girls' game was called 'Queen Anne'. Children stood in two facing lines. One line hid a ball amongst themselves. Both lines moved back and forth saying alternate lines of these verses:

Lady Queen Anne who sits in her stand
(sedan-chair)
And a pair of green gloves upon her hand,
As white as a lily, as fair as a Swan,
The fairest lady in a' the land.

Come smell my lily, come smell my rose,
Which of my maidens do you choose?
I choose you one, and I choose you all,
And I pray Miss (——) yield up the ball.

The ball is mine and none of yours,
Go to the woods and gather flowers;
Cats and kittens bide within,
But all young ladies walk out and in.

One child had to decide which child on the opposing side held the ball. If the guess was correct, the ball had to be given up.

55 Country children play at 'Blind Man's Bluff'.

Books

All children, rich and poor, were entertained
by nursery rhymes at an early age. Many
collections of these rhymes were published
during the second half of the century.
Tommy Thumb's Pretty Song Book (1744)
was an early favourite. Children's stories
were just beginning as picture books. Many
more books were published in the last 30
years of the century. The new children's
books were very moralizing. They tried to
make children obedient, hard-working, and
nature-loving. The books were often beauti-
fully illustrated. John Newbery's *Pretty
Little Pocket Book* published in 1742 was
very popular. A gimmick was used to help

sell this book: for an extra twopence, a ball
for the son or pin-cushion for the daughter
could be had with the book.

One hero was Dick Whittington. Another
was Giles Gingerbread, who learned his
letters by eating them (they were made of
gingerbread). Primrose Prettyface was the
heroine of a book published in 1783. She,
'by her sweetness of temper, and love of
learning, was raised from being the daughter
of a poor cottager to great riches, and the
dignity of lady of the manor'. In *Nurse
Lovechild's Legacy* 'Tom Trueby was a
good and sensible boy, who neither played
the truant nor kept company with naughty
children. . . he liked very well to play at ball
or top, and most particularly at marbles,
at which he was very clever, never cheated. . .'

67

56 *The First Stage of Cruelty* is the title of this 1750 engraving by Hogarth, in which children are shown torturing animals in various ways. The artist hoped to prevent cruelty by showing how disgusting it was to look at.

Children's books became much more plentiful by 1800 and also cheaper. There were many books available at 1d. Only the very poorest families could not afford these. One series published by Oliver and Boyd was called *Jack Dandy's Delight*. There were 40 at 6d, 26 at 2d, 40 at 1d, and 90 at ½d. John Harris followed Newbery's lead. In 1823 he published *Little Rhymes for Little Folk*. Stories that gave children warnings became popular: naughty children always ended up badly. The message to children was that they should be punctual, obedient, hard-working, honest and should not steal.

Kindness to the poor and to animals was encouraged in books of the late eighteenth

57 Boys rolling a hoop in Oxford in 1781. The boy on the right has a stick to keep the hoop rolling. Hoops were a favourite street toy.

58 Children's games have changed very little over the centuries. The 'Household Troops' prepare for battle, using watering cans and cooking pots as helmets, pot lids as shields, and gardening tools as swords. Children liked dressing up, and used everyday things in their games.

century and early 1800s. Children in the eighteenth century were very cruel to animals. Flies were stripped of their wings and birds of their feathers. Children neglected pets badly — or tormented them. Mrs Trimmer was one author who tried to teach children to be kinder to animals. Her *History of the Robins* was very famous, published in 1786.

Toys

Just as children's books were mainly to teach virtues, so many children's toys and games were meant to teach information and skills. Playing cards were used widely to teach all sorts of subjects. One pack even taught the basics of music. The jig-saw puzzle was first produced by John Spilsbury in 1762 for the teaching of geography. By the mid-1760s he had 30 different maps in jig-saw form for sale.

The first dice game in England, played on a painted board for instruction, was invented by John Jeffreys in 1759. This was called 'A Journey through Europe or the Play of Geography'. Players moved along a marked route according to the throw of the dice.

By the early nineteenth century there were many educational toys available. There were mechanical toys, such as water-mills and looms, which could be put together and made to work. There were cheap inflatable globes. There were toy theatres with movable scenery, Noah's Arks, animal farms, soldiers and forts, spinning tops. Dolls' houses and dolls included cheap cut-outs in paper with interchangeable clothes, and also fancy models with wax or earthenware faces, jointed bodies and large wardrobes. Rocking horses were also very popular. For babies there were simple rattles and teething rings.

While in 1730 there were no special toy shops, by 1780 toyshops were everywhere. At the end of the century the trade in children's toys and books was very large, and this in itself is proof that children in general were, for the first time, being treated with care and understanding, and with special attention to their individual needs.

59 Worthing beach at the end of the 18th century. Children enjoyed holidays by the sea, and young ladies would be wheeled to the edge of the water in bathing huts to take their morning swim.

Index

The numbers in **bold type** refer to the figure numbers of the illustrations